Foreign Matter & Other Poems

Also by Ouyang Yu and published by Ginninderra Press
Terminally Poetic

Ouyang Yu

Foreign Matter
& Other Poems

Foreign Matter & Other Poems
ISBN 978 1 76109 393 7
Copyright © text Ouyang Yu 2022
Cover image: painting by Simon Cee, photographed by the author

First published 2022 by
Ginninderra Press
PO Box 3461 Port Adelaide 5015
www.ginninderrapress.com.au

Contents

Foreign Matter	7
Writing Poetry: An Un-Australian Activity (a sequence)	**9**
The White Australian	11
Fragments of an Evening Walk in Kingsbury	15
A Job Advertisement in China	17
Anecdotes from Life	**19**
Lines Written at the Melbourne Mental (a sequence)	**31**
Citizenship (a sequence)	**41**
When I Have Not One Friend to Think of	43
Cultural Relics	44
The Story of a Telephone	45
The Other Eye	47
Invading Australia (a sequence)	**49**
Lines of Least Resistance (a sequence)	**59**
Who's Afraid of Les Murray	61
Reviews of My Unpublished Book	62
Subtleties	63
An English Professor's Complaint	65
Family Life: A Portrait (a sequence)	**67**
Going Home (a sequence)	**75**
The House Problem	77
Home	78
On an Autumn Day in April	79
Spring Festival, 1994	80
An Australian Dream (a sequence)	**83**
An Australian Dream	85
After an Interview	86
Triple Standards	88

Untitled	89
Career Counselling to a Student of English	90
Goodbye, Australia – from a Chinese student (a sequence)	**91**
Diary of a Crazy Contemporary Convict	93
The Last Barrier	98
They Have Married White Men	99
How Many Years Does It Take to Become an Australian?	101
Sojourners?	102
Poetry Unemployed (a sequence)	103
City in Waiting	107
Rediscovered Poems	**109**
'no i won't go back to china he told me'	111
The Poet's Wife (2)	113
On an Australia Day	114
'the west in the whale'	115
'how is one going to change himself'	116
The Chinese Way of Writing	118
'I often wonder about them'	119
After Colonisation	120
Colonised	122
The Lonely Man	123
Farting	124
For Christmas in the Year of the Bird	125
An Old Classmate Visits My Melbourne Home	126
The Sky	128
A Simple Mathematical Equation	129
Self-titled	130
My Heart	131
Simile	132
Acknowledgements	133

Foreign Matter

《异物》

1、珍奇的东西
2、特指稀有的美食
3、不同之事；其他事物
4、指其他事因
5、怪物。指妖魔鬼怪之类
6、指已死的人
7、特指人死后遗体
8、指人类以外的生物

Foreign Matter

1. Rare and exotic things
2. Rare delicacies, specifically
3. Different matters and other matters
4. Cause of other matters
5. Strange matters, in the category of demons and monsters
6. The dead
7. The remains of a person after death, specifically
8. Beings beyond humanity

(This is a found poem, its Chinese version based on this website, known as 'Baidu Baike', or Baidu Encyclopedia: https://baike.baidu.com/item/异物/3495008. Translated by the author.)

Writing Poetry:
An Un-Australian Activity
(a sequence)

The White Australian

is a nameless guy in asia
he travels with a face borrowed from europe
he is careful not to allow his melbourne or sydney
accent to show through
and he has a good reason:
they wouldn't understand it
if i do not speak like an english or american
he is an intellectual
you know

not many people know or care
about australia
he is too lazy to explain
better pretend to be something you are not
and get better treatment

is a woman
and feels very superior
'cause she comes from a democracy
sometimes mispronounced by her stupid students
as demoncrazy
she would then grow justly indignant
and deplore the lack of sanitation and education
as well as too much hospitality
designed she said
to deceive
she'd sometimes show off her feminism
again sometimes mispronounced as famileechm
by refusing the friendly offer of a male hand
or by taking any bewildered boy students
to task
for daring to crack jokes with her
it is sad however
to see her back

to normal
in her native land australia
where she speaks in subdued tones
very demure and coy

is a writer
who becomes interested
doesn't know the language
and is not going to worry about it
the country abounds in cheap efficient interpreters
they not he
are going to provide him with the info
necessary to his master
pisses
he's got the imagination
he wouldn't be bothered with facts
he is a fictionist someone good at intertextuality

at other times
he is a university administrator
he is not happy with the present state of affairs
at the heart of hearts
too many asians
who do bring in a lot of money
but not as many manners
and respect
they should be kept in their right place
especially the male:
factories fruit and vegetable markets grocery stores
milk bars takeaway restaurants
as secretaries as telephone receptionists as library assistants
at best as foremen as students even phd
but not he thought to himself
as university lecturers except to teach in their own language

the administrator was as inscrutable as ever
when he had just done the interview
in which an asian appeared
the decision came out fair and square:
he didn't get it because others had better qualifications
or more experience
while his secret thought was:
that guy should really congratulate himself on being shortlisted

is a literary editor
who is highly proficient in deciphering identities of names
this is a chinese pretending to write in bad english
that is an indonesian struggling with right diction
that is obviously someone from vietnam
who has not even learnt his basics in grammar
he can get around his political correct corner however
by picking something from within the commonwealth
some sri lankan some indian someone who learned english as a baby
though under a different skin
in the end the editor is triumphant:
the quality of english is ensured
and so is the purity

at home he is different
he defines himself and others by the strange word
un-australian
as if it is not in their nature to be bad
which only the un-australian can do

is everywhere
who is only skin deep
s/he smiles with body
never eyes
s/he is nice when you first meet

like a trained air stewardess
there is no hope of becoming their friends
just as there is no hope of them becoming us
because they like their borrowed mothers in england
imitated fathers in america
and blood brothers in europe

is fond of pretty words

but don't accuse him of being a racist
he is not
he doesn't look like one
he isn't one of those blaineys howards diques hansons
he is only a white
australian

too right

(Geoffrey Blainey is the Australian historian who has published an anti-Asian book *All for Australia* (1984); John Howard was prime minister of Australia who made anti-Asian remarks in 1988; John Dique is the author of an anti-Asian book *Immigration: the Quiet Invasion* (1985); and Pauline Hanson, head of anti-Asian One Nation Party in Australia.)

Fragments of an Evening Walk in Kingsbury

it was a hot evening, windless
the grass
half dead, white with rustling noise underneath
the boy suggested that you go out for a walk
you did
the three of you, walking listlessly towards a park beyond the houses

two women went past us
across the street
their averted eyes and their dog running ahead of them
nose held on a string
elicited from you a comment
about the inapproachability of the such likes
and she agreed by saying that they were all the same
neither worse nor better
being human beings

all the while
the eucalyptus standing tall and dark-green
against a darkness
that was gathering behind darkened
mute houses
the boy wondered if he could go and sit on the gilded edge
of the bank of cloud and enjoyed the sunlight from there
the mother said it was only air
and you the useless
sitting on the wooden fence
watching the cloud change shape
as it always does everywhere in the world

suddenly the silent streets seemed startled
when they heard you say:
i don't like australia
i don't like china, either

the boy's mother paused, then said,
that's right
i don't like china, either
curious isn't it
how beautiful they had thought of australia
before they came here

you watched the cloud turn into a pistol
pointed at you and said with longing:
if only i could have a river here
and stroll along its water and sun-filled bank

as you approached your rented home
rank with wilful weeds
you heard your heart echoing an old unpublished line of your own:

how i want to go away
to anywhere else

A Job Advertisement in China

come to australia
a great country for you:

you'll find factories galore
where you'll enjoy the standard multiculturalism
that i'm sure you have never seen before
malaysians vietnamese yugoslavians thais romanians macedonians
and do whatever you like to do:
carving chickens washing dishes sweeping the floor
making socks shoes donuts dimsins and dildoes
don't complain
for don't you know australia is a workingmen's paradise?

if you've got qualifications it's even better
you could possibly work in a primary or secondary school
as a lote teacher teaching australian kids how to say
ni hao ma or *cao ni ma*

mind you: your english has got to improve
regardless of your qualifications
you know how the saying goes:
it is never too old to learn?
so it is never too chinese or asian to learn english

come to australia all of you
we've got so much freedom
in fact a prisonful of it

and don't forget to contact refugee review tribunal
or noosr or racv or social security or ces or your nearest police station
if anything unexpected happens

next it could be you

lote: language other than English
ni hao ma: how are you?
cao ni ma: fuck your mother
noosr: National Organisation for Overseas Students' Review
racv: Royal Automobiles Centre of Victoria
ces: Council of Adults Education

Anecdotes from Life

(which should be told in Chinese but have to be told in English, beginning from 9 May 1993)

1

he is going back
he has already bought a ticket
why in such haste
because he is sick
of and in australia
his girl has left him a catholic girl
whose parents object to her marrying a non-catholic
oh the most beautiful girl in his factory in his work group
another man also loves her a yugoslavian
but she prefers him you have seen him you know what a fine young
man he is
having obtained a b.a. in philosophy
taller than most of the chinese
but her parents just don't allow her to marry him
such stubborn people so backward in outlook so unenlightened in thinking
the girl has to quit the factory to quit him
but even in china no parents can stop their girls marrying the men
                                        they want to marry absolutely none
it's incredible that such things can still happen in a country
that claims itself progressive and free
i suppose what is at work is
the damned white supremacy

2

i lived in the states for one year and a half you know
but for the scholarship i got here i would not have come
america is a much better place oh definitely much better
never like this
so desolate after dark not even a ghost to be seen
well i stayed in new york you know columnbia university
to be frank just about everything is better
no racism no the sort of thing that happened in los angeles is too rare
it is so easy to make money even in recession
you can always find a casual job for five or six dollars an hour
not too little considering the cheap board and lodging
and the people are so nice when i arrived i had with me two big
suitcases weighing 30 kilograms each and when i got up the stairs in
the subway people behind me stopped to let me pass and when i
reached the school dormitory there were a lot of people helping me
carry them i was really moved
even a tiny little detail like passing through the customs makes a lot
of difference in the states nobody checked my things but in
tullamarine airport they checked through my stuff so thoroughly like
x-ray that i felt transparent and i was made to look a bitter fool when
they commented coolly on my rice cooker
nobody here would give you a hand you know
what i think about it?
i think australians don't really like us chinese or asians yes that's right i
know what you mean exactly it is a bit like squeezed between
super-powers made to constantly feel uneasy and impotent but still
persistent in the belief in their own damned superiority that is only a poor
shadow of the past inherited from their great british brutish forefathers
what my suggestion to make the country powerful?
well easy enough more people
more and more people that's all

and opening up special economic zones
to allow for intense economic competition and to put down a few airs
regarding their easy and lazy
ways of life
well who knows anyway these days?

3

to tell you the truth i haven't made love to an australian woman ever since i came to australia and i haven't even thought of fucking one to me they look all the same are simply too ugly repellent smelly dressed awkwardly behaving strangely like a man that's what really pissed me off you know however i did get fucked one bright morning when i was going to the city i was sitting by the window the 256 stopped somewhere near the shopping mall and my casual glance out the window caught a group of teenagers lolling nearby what are they doing at such an early hour it was around eight you know then i recalled that it was time for school just when i took my glance back i saw this fat masculine girl holding out her hairy hand with all the fingers closed up and only the middle finger thrust out like an abnormal clitoris at me AT ME but the bus was already moving away and the abnormal clitoris nailed in my innocent eyes and i regretted to myself i had not even had time to retaliate by doing some exhibitionist trick of showing her my oriental rooster or root i often thought of that in my later days in australia

the other day i was turning into a parking lot in my camira i didn't notice another car also turning into it from the opposite side i decided not to give way and as i was easing myself between the two white lines i found the same fucking gesture that the yellow-haired ape – for that lass did look an ape to me – held up for me muttering something with her tiny hole of a mouth that never showed the upper teeth she was gone but the middle finger that protruded through the windowpane stood like another weird clitoris haunting me still today funny isn't it again the other day when i can't remember exactly the same sort of fucking gesture was poked at me again and again and again from a guy who almost jumped out his window at me for i saw him in my interior rear mirror and without thinking my own left hand went off the wheel its middle finger standing out facing his way over my shoulder sure that it could catch his fucking eyes it did while my car was turning another round-about then lost him my wife said he was half out of his window shouting obscenities i said did you see him she said yes and my son said yes i saw him with a mane of red hair i said in chinese fuck his mother's cunt and fuck his ancestors whoever they were and my wife tried to stop me saying it's not nice to say these things in your son's presence and i said i know it's not but it's even less nice to do these things in the presence of foreigners like us in australia did we ever do that to any foreigners in china?

4

where are all the australians
after a few years he wonders to himself
all the people he met are NOT australians:
the guy who runs the grocery store across the street
is from yugoslavia whose son the big-headed one once said to him in
answer to his question why cigarettes were so expensive in australia:
This is not China This is Australia
how did he bloody know i am chinese we never even exchanged a question
he wondered
which pissed him off and he never even looked at the b(p)ig-head again
the guy who let the house to him is from bulgaria
the woman who runs the milk bar is from vietnam who was
infuriated with his second ignorant inquiry about liquor:
I told you before:
This is not a liquor store This is a milk bar
in a voice not too friendly
the guy sitting next to him with a dark lean face in a poetry reading revealed
to him at the end that he was an SCM (spanish-chinese-malaysian)
the woman who introduced him to radio audience introduced herself
as polish-jewish
the guy for whom he worked some time as a kitchen-hand is a
malaysian-chinese who pays him 30 dollars for 8 hours who thinks the guy
across the street who runs a pizza store is too stupid
his wife comes back with the story that when they have tea time all the
factory divides into groups of different nationalities
turkish talking to turkish vietnamese to vietnamese chinese to chinese
yugoslavs to yugoslavs

where are all the australians
he often wonders
until one day he bumped into this real australian who says he's born
in australia
he's some sort of politician claiming some knowledge of asia etc
he had an argument with him
he always had since then
with genuine australians
for genuine australians are always very bigoted people
who don't watch tv who think they are better than anyone else in the world
who is afraid of competition
who hates other people talking too much
about themselves who –
but the argument was he remembers about whether australia was really
a country at all
he said that from a chinese point of view
it was not
it was a fake country
because first of all
it has an english flag and celebrates an english queen's birthday
so that when you want to become an australian citizen you swear
allegiance to the queen and you become instead queen's subjects
can you imagine he asked a chinese swearing allegiance to an emperor
excavated from an ancient tomb
secondly your country is fake because you don't have your own national
language
you speak write and think english and if you do that you are not really
australian you are english that is why even today you pride yourself on
english-awarded degrees english-awarded prizes english-awarded
honours english-awarded people and now you lean to the other side you
watch too much american you cover too much american in your media
you drink too much coke pepsi you eat too much macdonald too much kfc
and you shit too
much american

but you never seem to have your own soul your genuine self
you are always either english or american or some such things
how sad
and thirdly the most funny thing is after two hundred years
you still regard yourself as european
where are you really
you are close to the antarctica
that's all i know of
no you are not part of asia nor of europe nor of america
if you want to gain independence
you have to be yourself
australia in a place that is none of those things
but is called oceania
the guy of course did not agree with him for you know
genuine australians
never agree with anybody even if they know they are wrong
they don't even like to hear it pointed out to them that they are wrong
but that is that i don't care
australia has to rely on something you know
either english or america or china or indonesia or india
it can never rely on itself
sure thing

5

that night you told me that you do not belong to any class at all in australia you manage to live in a vacuum using everything second hand is this a second-hand country or what? you often wonder you even feel like a second-hand man but you obviously know the metaphor that australia is full of second-hand europeans as chinese you probably are not even second-hand you are third-hand fourth-hand last-hand or multiple-hand already you are pissed off by this second-hand fact

but i told you that it's all right to be second-hand you at least have something first hand right? your freedom

you said fuck off freedom which is meant only for the rich that can buy freedom is not for life but for sale you said you've got to think about life some more you said you've been thinking all the while

but i told you to have a look at the way ordinary australians live like they sleep like innocent animals on the lawn in the sun on sundays without a shadow of nightmares of war or famine or disaster or revolution without even imagining it they exercise their life away in gymnasiums criss-cross with shining steel instruments building up postcolonial muscles…

to what purpose? you interrupted and continued, only to be spent in shit or love or drinking reveries or writing books for the body hardly ever for the mind you said that's the problem with australians you know

i said that's the problem with all the rich peaceful countries mate they have got so much time and money and energy to spend that they become perverse and think perhaps to be a bit stupid is good

well what's the point of criticising as long as you can lead a peaceful life even if it is poor both of you wondered as chinese you know what that really means

you don't want to think no more

Lines Written at the Melbourne Mental (a sequence)

i want to go home
home i want to go
from this place that
makes me mad and low

1

winter again
the sea at port phillip bay
is muddy fury
the sky
over the melbourne mental
an unbroken grey
rain is spitting
and spitting
its cold unconcern
unto the wind-screen
of my second eye
near the intensive care ward
cars shoot past
in a hurry to leave for home
leaving behind them
a world of night
as dark as melbourne

2

they told me it was okay to be here
they said you were fine
all you do is stay for a couple of days
no worry they said
just tell us what's the problem
i said no problem
i want to go home
they said
this is home
it is literally a HOME
i said i knew nobody here
i did not see my friends
i did not see my parents
i did not see sisters or brothers
how can it be a home
they said don't worry
it will be a home
if you stay long enough
i wondered if it was like a tree
where any birds can live
but don't birds have a recognised home to go back to
do they just fly away
never to return
like bullets do
or do they
like my heart
once centrifugalised
go into a seeking cycle

3

nights refuse to go away
with their imaginary darkness
my HOME-mates sleep away their time
before a wasteful TV
i was very light-headed
and could not speak
the medicine was circulating in all the creeks
of my blood vessels
like a poisonous snake
whose tongue
was my tongue
whose eyes
were my eyes
and whose body
was my body
i crept up to my psychiatric doctor
and hissed
with a voice loaded with venom
so he diagnosed maximum security
and i thought wordlessly
that it was good for me to breed

4

occasionally
flashes of memory would break out
like fresh diseases:

a big river that flows from the top of a green hill
a surging ocean of white clouds that are holding my plane hostage
a temple that fades in the setting sun

nothing to do with australia
where a rented lodging
was disintegrating
in the afternoon perfection

5

i said i didn't speak english
so they got me an interpreter
who knew my language
i suppose this poem is what he had written about me
the bastard
taking advantage of my pain
and my devious disease
he didn't even tell me that he was intending to home me
in this poem
he may capture my soul
but how could he house my body
restless
in a lot of words

6

my doctors were all australians
white and refined
trained, sure of themselves
and determined
to put me right
in front of modern technology
and an efficient culture
that i used to worship from another continent
i still do
although i can't help see double
tremble even when i don't want to
die a daily death under the effect
of strong medical weaponry
and wake up to see a white refined hospital home

7

my god disappears with blue-eyed angels
that once accompanied me on a purifying journey
in which i drank tap water a hundred times a day
to ethnically cleanse myself
i now see a landscape turning yellow
with wattles
little nameless flowers that were soon done away with
on a constantly mown lawn
much advertised pages
that were weighing heavy
on their commercial dreams
and a melbourne sun
that was as golden
as my psychological imagination
home away
homed in

Citizenship
(a sequence)

When I Have Not One Friend to Think of

the question repeats itself:

why am i here
why are they here
what have we got to do with it all

the night becomes colder with increasing unconcern
the house
like it has always been
listens to the gibberish keyings of an irrelevant computer

outside
the world dies its deadest death

Cultural Relics

in a hundred years
these things would be unobtainable:

the white flowers of toilet paper
wrapping up the whitest sperm
just culled from her blossoming thighs
encircling her night-black stilettos

a list of names that you've spent a whole day inventing
otherland northern wolf southern bird
before you settled down for something more conventional
that posterity could only find in a microfilm

old clothes that showed change of time
and yourself and are now consciously resisting
the onslaught of the foreign
eye

and this blunt little scissors
that you had bought you cannot remember where in china
years ago
and were using to keep pruning away at yawning jaws

the academic researcher of the next century
when turning over the fragile pages of this rare collection
what would s/he find among windows of classifieds
or ant-like letters of news
what would s/he know of this man
typing before his macintosh classic ii
trying to fax the summer
back to a place he used to call home

The Story of a Telephone

why don't they call me
you said

but why don't you call them first?
she said

if they don't call me first
i won't call them first

but why should they call you
if you don't call them

it's not fair
for i have called some of them

but it's holiday
they might call you back some time

they never do
they always seem to wait for me to call them

well if you feel that way
why don't you simply call them

only strangers call me these days
marketing people salespersons promoters

you do have people calling you
don't you

but they talk rubbish
they keep talking rubbish

then you are better off
without getting any calls

how i wish my telephone kept ringing
and i got calls from everywhere everyday

but you are unemployed
who wants to call a useless person

(already you saw in your mind's eye that you snatched your telephone from its root and smashed it into pieces and heard imaginary people trying in vain to get through and yourself laughing heartily and saying serve them right)

never mind, you said
we shall keep hoping that one of these days they will come to us

they the already non-existent
the hollow the empty the self-happy?

you wondered

The Other Eye

when i was getting in the clothes aired on the umbrella wires in the garden
the other eye watched me
through its post/colonial window
curtains
saying in admiration
one must really have such guys for mates
for they are so womanly

when i was backing my car out of the driveway slightly clumsily
my front wheel rolling over the curb
the other eye turned away to the grass being cut beneath
its noisy lawnmower
thinking to him/herself:
these people are really no good at such things

so it was the same when i let my garden overrun with flower-dotted grass
for the other eye would simply show contempt
for such heathenish practice
or snort at my sometimes yelling to the boy
ughhhhhhhhhhhh
those bloody cruel animals

the other eye is omnipresent
wherever you go
whatever you do
it keeps its vigil over you
wordlessly

until you see it yourself
in your heart:

an eye white

Invading Australia
(a sequence)

1

z called me this morning

he came here a few months ago, then he disappeared
i sort of knew what he would call me about
it would be about invasion
invading australia
an idea he got from reading my book
although i told him to ring me back one hour later
as i had not even brushed my teeth or washed my face

2

sure enough, he said he would design a website
called "yellow peril"
he would then invite people from all over the world
"you mean the chinese-speaking world?"
i queried and commented that it wouldn't do
as to maintain it from month to month would cost too much
and then to set up something just for the chinese was simply not
worth
it

3

'what then do you think you could do?' z said
i said, i've got an idea and it was this:
invite everyone including your state premier
to your opening at an empty gallery
fill it to overflowing and just when they start wondering
why there's nothing happening
get your troop of chinese soldiers wearing pla uniforms
carrying their rifles with ice-shining bayonets
marching into the open gallery and announcing the arrest
of all the important vips and meanwhile announcing on the radio
you had brought in and placed in a corner
that australia had been taken over by new china
exactly the same way as described in a novel written by an australian
and published in the 1980s
'brilliant idea,' z said, 'but i do not have the heart to do such
things
to such an innocent people!'

4

'so far,' z said, 'all they do is to be looked at, gazed at
to have their wounds exposed and examined'
'right,' i said. 'from now on, with my idea of invasion of australia
we'll look at them and trample over them, all over them'
i then said to him that he could get the people held in detention centres
as extras to appear in his show
my ideas rushing in and i started talking about this being
gazed-at-ness
saying, right! it's like mai tongku: selling your misery
to please them because they, you know, are crazy about being beaten up
they pay for you to piss on them shit on them and spit on them
and get a hell lot of pleasure out of it
in the end they are the masters and you are the slaves
see what i mean?

5

the best thing, i said, is hold the exhibition in the parliament
house
in canberra and set shop selling all the memorabilia
commemorating chinese soldiers who have sacrificed their lives
in building new china and erasing the name of australia from the face
of
the earth
and everyone having a good laugh out of it all

6

the only thing to mind is, i said, the future success of such an
adventure
if you go it alone, i wouldn't participate but if we do it together
we'd have to have an equal share of proceeds from the sales
the admissions and the prize-money
etc, chouhua shuozai qiantou, as Chinese saying goes
'say the ugly words right at the beginning' z repeated it
and, for my readership, i make it more australian below:
set the terms right at the start to avoid any future
misunderstandings
or unequal share of the booty

7

i have one more idea about this invasion show:
issue 10,000 visitor's visas to as many beautiful girls from china
get them to come to australia and visited by australian males
don't be offended
it's just a show
'what about the grant?' z said
'what about it?' i said
'australians always support good ideas that they like
you probably will get it but i'm not sure'

8

just at this junction an email drifted in from china:
'australia is an old man's country; i can't live there
thank you for all your kindness while i was there
but i've decided i prefer the noise and dirt here'

Lines of Least Resistance
(a sequence)

Who's Afraid of Les Murray

let's face it
multiculturalism is for the ethnics
not the likes of you

who do not know a word of the foreign languages
who do not write a word for the other
who do not have a word that can be put across

you are out in this new edition of multicultural australia
you are down with the onslaught of this new kind of english
that you can't judge with your dating authority

you can be your own editor
and edit yourself in and out of history
to stand in a world that no one cares to read

just listen to this single person here
powerless against the likes of you
speaking in a multicultural voice:

who's afraid of les murray?

Reviews of My Unpublished Book

how can a chinese write in english
and about australia
the australian professor of english was genuinely offended
it's our language
not his
you know
he would not allow himself to be angry though
because those ethnics are not worth getting angry about
but the fact that a chinese writes in english
and even gets published
is really a sore

the well published australian author is also unhappy
for most of the day on which he heard the news
he sulked over the matter
someone who came from china now writes in english
probably in a couple of years will publish even more than him
that's incredible
that such people should not be allowed more opportunities
must be made clear to the editor:
these people are simply opportunists
who take advantage of our multicultural policy
and will eventually take over our english language
when it will become chinglish instead
if you know what i mean

others remain unperturbed
thinking to themselves:
get fucked you bloody chinks and chows
you won't become anything by writing our language
no congratulations for you mate
not worth it

or as les/s proposes and praises:

go for the australian prizes
not the ethnic ones

Subtleties

1

i laughed heartily
when my son imitated the voice of a man
he put to be in his fifties
who said this to him one day:

every toime you biounced that ball
you maike me headache
you bloody nuisence bloody nuisence
piss off

i'd ask him to say it again and again
forgetting in my merriment over the accent
to tell him how to talk back

2

it was only when i came back
and told her in our language about what had just happened
that the meaning became meaningful for the first time

he said that this mouse trap i could only use it once
for when it caught one the others wouldn't come
just like if you yourself were one big rat and got killed
on the trap the big unsmiling fellow broke into a grin
the other people like you would never come

i remembered i laughed at that
when she stopped me with a:
he was so insolent!

to this day i still recall the incident
with an imaginary statement to this effect:
that's not a nice comparison, mite!
and try to conjure up the consequence

3

i don't remember what i did
but i flicked the red rental card onto the counter
and it flew back over the counter onto where my feet were
my blood rose
and i said i am not going to pick it up unless you do
the hairy man's mouth moved in the shape of a fuck
their national abuse
and he was edging away from the counter towards my direction

later on
she'd always use it as an example of how cowardly i was
in the face of an approaching fight
not man enough she said
to stand still there and fight it on
but run away from it all

i don't think i have an answer to that

An English Professor's Complaint

well they don't write good english do they
these people who come from elsewhere
i don't understand why they keep doing what they are doing
so incompetently
do they think by somehow writing english
they can become english and then us
do they think that they can eventually run the country
with the bad english they are speaking and writing
even their grammar is accented
r's for l's
de for the
no verbs no plural no articles
and this student should have the cheek to suggest
that eventually we are going to adopt a language
called australian
how semantically etymologically and linguistically unacceptable
australians can possibly speak australian
just as americans or canadians can speak american or canadian
australians have got to speak english
their mother tongue
their mother's tongue

australians speak english
and english are australians
that's all i know and need to know

and i am a professor of english
not of a multicultural language
called australian

Family Life: A Portrait
(a sequence)

1

often when he heard the purring of the engine
on the driveway
and the final pulling of the handbrake
he was at his computer
wondering what to do to finish
a broken poem
or what words to use
to strip the piece of verbosity

then she came in
with the white plastic bag
that contained her lunch box her driver's licence her car key
having long given up her different bags
black red and brown
bought from myer k-mart or one of the garage sales

she would stand there
closing her eyes and said
i am tired
and he would take her and her heavy sigh
in his arms
smelling her factory
and said
rest here baby

2

the dinner was usually three dishes
plus rice
yesterday it was
bamboo-leaf vegetables sautéd with cantonese sausages
plain green cauliflowers
and braised drumsticks
today it was
a braised red fish that neither of them could name
sliced potatoes sautéd with salt and pepper
and shredded bean curd and shredded radish
sautéd with shredded ham
the son at once said that the last one was good
the father praised that the son had a good palate
the son did not hear clearly and said
what i did not have a good taste
the mother explained that your father praised you for having a good tongue
finally when the dinner was eaten
and the mother went away to the sitting room
he heard her say:
i never did enjoy the dinner that i prepared myself
i'd wish that someone could do that for me
if only for once
and his son joked about the fish
saying you and mother saw the fish
mother said we buy it
you said no it's too dear
then you saw a cheap one
and you bought it
then we all eat rubbish

3

then came the great moment for him
for this was the last day of her period
only yesterday she had said to him
promisingly
just wait one more day
i'd be ready
and now he ordered
the boy must go to bed early
she must wash before him
and he must turn the heater on
which most of the time he had left cold
when he was trying to finish writing his diary
while having his feet soaked in hot water
her voice came soft from the bedroom
don't hurry –
it was soon over
and he was lying heavy over her
before she threw him down
and said
i'd go to the toilet
today
it was only today
that he heard her comment
i had not enjoyed it at all
not for a second
it was all for you

4

occasionally he'd become agitated
and get out all the old manuscripts
and start looking for addresses
muttering to himself
i'd fill in all those bloody holes
see how many stamps i have got
oh there are seven left
and she
knitting her sweater
forever knitting
taking it to be her most luxurious pastime
would say to him:
you cranky poet
they'd not even look at your stuff
you are just wasting your money time and life
remember?
a poet is better to die than live
after sealing all the seven envelops
with saliva
he went to her and put his mouth
immediately against her throat
making a sucking noise
and said
tonight i'll fill your envelope

5

but there is nothing more intriguing than her story
of how she said goodmorning to a group of three
smoking right in front of the factory entrance
and was not greeted back
how she thought it was so insulting that
she vowed that she'd never greet them again
he commented: you should not even have paid any attention
to those bastards
in the first place
she said but you never know when they did what they did
sometimes when you did not greet them
they greeted you of their own accord
they were crazy people
no, he corrected her
they were no more crazy than you and i
you know what
they just had this power over you
that they thought they could do whatever they wanted to do to you
if they did not want to return your greetings they did not do it
if they did greet you you had to greet back
is not that what you often did?
she became silent
and i told her how i hated being looked at
by these insolent people's possessing eyes
and mouths
that silently stare at you
very sittingly
that spit out comments
when you are within imagining distance

6

then she talked about her own country
which was also his own country
and wondered how long one could go home to live
after one got his or her p.r.
he said that he'd never go back again
not for a single day
but why, she asked
you were so frustrated by this degrading country
where so many people were unfriendly no even hostile
where so many people had wished you far far away
why wasn't home a better place at all
he heard himself say
to himself
well wife
there was no home
no more home than where we were
you had only to look at the death in my eyes to know it
then he heard wife say
you'd better die
as a poet
for nowhere fits you

(p.r. refers to permanent resident status in Australia.)

Going Home
(a sequence)

The House Problem

i don't know why i always feel sad
when i hear someone is buying a house
or has bought one
it's not that i'm jealous of their wealth
or of their courage in living well first
nor is it that i fear the trouble one has to go into in doing such a thing

i guess there is something wrong with my mind
which keeps warring me against taking roots in one place
a house it says is a death
you buy death and live in it
that's what it's all about

i often wonder if my body is not my already house
like a snail
the easiest and the lightest i've ever got
that i can take with me
even to the moon
given a spaceship chance
and death is certainly a permanent house
that forever awaits me
even when i can't afford to pay
for its long-term lease

but i still do not know why i feel so sad
whenever i think of my body as a house

Home

1

the boy ends every one of his writing assignments with
'so i go home'
i can't say that
even if i am at home
knowing that my home is still far away
which is not what it was or is
but like a dream that exists
in the closed eyes

2

they look exactly like us
with black eyes black hair and yellow faces
one thing will set us apart:
if something happens
we all have a home to return to
but they'll have to stay

On an Autumn Day in April

it was a grey day like today
three years ago
in australia

when i looked out the plane window
down at a landscape of most melancholy colours
brown dark without relief of water

i couldn't have imagined that i would be sitting before
a screen as grey as that day today
trying to see through it all

to my day of coming
then china had just begun to die
now australia is still far away

john had told me in his letter to china
how beautiful the autumn was
all i could see was enormous grey-haired grass and other trees

but the new letter from china tells me
how he misses australia for its sun and blue sky and green grass
when he is back to shanghai unable to get out of it or of his cold

and all i remember is
the sensual cherry trees on the luojia hill showering their snow blossoms
just for multicoloured high heels to pierce through

(The Luojia Hill is where Wuhan University is located in Wuhan, China.)

Spring Festival, 1994

1

even spring festival
does not mean anything to me
any more

having lived 36 of it
in china
it's good for a change here

without the hell-splitting
noise of crackers
without worrying who/m to visit

on the first day
no more reunion
with the family

parents of both sides
brothers and sisters
and the ever growing kids

all gathered for the 30th of the big year
with its food of all varieties
and indefinite length

but here i am
in a house deserted
by a school-attending boy

and a factory-working wife
trying to think of something to do
in a long hot summer

with nothing much to do
when someone called in
and said, it's new year's eve

2

we waited until 10
while it was seven back at home
time they must be watching the seven p.m. news from cctv
then i picked up the phone and dialled the number
001186 713 353007
and i wondered about the wonders of such human achievements
while waiting for it to get through
not without some jamming and confusing and recorded message
my father's voice came struggling over:
i am good
i know you ring to say hello

and i said happy new year
my son said happy new year
my wife said happy new year
until there wasn't much left unsaid
when i thought of something and told father to listen to the next day's
radio australia between 8 and 10 p.m. beijing time
'cause there would be my recorded message of good new year wishes to him
and others

3

on the first day of the chinese spring festival
it was as quiet at kingsbury as anywhere else in australia
except for a neighbouring lawnmower
that was as busy as a bee
buzzing like an incessant fly against the window

my wife had just called the factory to say that she could not go to work
today because she wasn't feeling well
but my son had to go to school
the education system was so horrific in australia
that loss of one day at school
would mean loss of our temper

but i had other things to do
so she was left alone
celebrating the occasion by herself
writing unfinished letters home

(The Western version of Spring Festival is Chinese New Year.)

An Australian Dream
(a sequence)

An Australian Dream

$360 a fortnight from social security
probably $380
if you have a family
plus a kid

no work
play all day
enjoy yourself

australian dream
easy
and

cheap

After an Interview

the decision is being made
when the bus is turning a street corner
reminiscent of a raucous interviewer

the decision is being made
when the bus-taker and the driver
are half-awake and dreaming

and the afternoon sun
is relentless through the moving window
striking on the burning hair of the dreamer

the decision is being made
somewhere in a building
well used to an exclusive process of high standard

in the city where
women are lovely but refuse to be part of the dream
the bus-taker dreams

where the decision is being made
in the conspiracy of knowing smiles
in the prepared lists of interrogation

designed to create failures
the decision is being made
while australia is moving

towards asia
the decision is being made
while australia

is moving asian
the decision is being made
while the bus-taker goes home

remembering his answer
that in total poverty
he chooses to live

and the welcoming smile
on the faces of readily consenting
males and females

the decision is being made
against him
who has left his home in asia

Triple Standards

mother to son:

don't act like an australian
they don't have homework
they are lazy
that's why they are stupid
and that's why they are insolent
as long as you are my son
you'll have to do homework
in everything:
maths physics (oh no they don't even teach that in primary school)
english chinese painting
you can't grow up a stupid australian like them
you have to learn how to be intelligent

husband to wife:

yes i get good pay
i always do
you know they pay you well
they don't really care
they can afford to
that's one good thing about them
far better than your countrymen
and mine
they are the worst lot in this
i'd rather be a slave to them
than to them

husband and wife and son
they spend their holidays with themselves
or their friends from their old country

Untitled

in this new country
i am feeling very old

my ancient face
frozen in time

is wrought in the shape
of a question

but why the new world
is so old

with all the familiar features
of a corrupted notion

why the heart
of the new world

is so old
with the cunning of a craftsman

must this continent be
but a second-hand car

newly painted and reconditioned
for the sunday market

must this world be
an ageless whore

experienced to the utmost
employable degree…

i am feeling old
in this as-new country

Career Counselling to a Student of English

i know you are speaking good english
in fact you speak better english than most australians
i mean certainly most chinese
you can even write well
you write creatively which is fantastic
with your background
you ARE employable
as a translator and interpreter
on an on-call basis
oh i see that would be a different matter
well it might be worth a try
yeees you certainly can
our universities are all eeo now
although not like the u.s. unis
where it is written into the constitution
that ethnic minority people and women
are welcome and encouraged
ours are better i'd say
and fairer as expressed in our national anthem
because we don't have to say that
i mean because we don't have this sort of problem
we don't have to provide for it
see?
anyway i don't see why you can't
as the saying goes
take the opportunity by the forelock
if there isn't any
you can take the forelock by the opportunity
it's all the same

i'm not joking
give australia is my advice
if you'd pursue
what you have been studying

//
Goodbye, Australia
– from a Chinese student
(a sequence)

Diary of a Crazy Contemporary Convict

1

i know i'm near insane
the january heat drives me nuts
days and days of talking to myself
and the computer
of losing temper with my beloved
of refusing and refusing to contact anyone
of my own free accord
have produced these effects on me
that i no longer think i can love
but i have a hatred as wide as
the sky and the earth

that i'm a contemporary convict
sent from china by my former self
to spend a life of imprisoning freedom
and of boredom by time
and end my life in total
sterility and obscurity

2

sometimes i dream of derailing a train
full of empty seats and lights

sometimes i dream of lying across
princes highway or hume highway

to hold up hours of traffic
until run over or shot dead by the bullet-police

sometimes i'd love to make love to a genuine australian woman
    right in front of myer or katies or david jones
just to hear her say that i am loved

sometimes i did kill a few people
    in my dreams

they all turn out to be prudish academics
who are so fucking quiet in and about things

putting covers of new books on their bloody doors
faking a smile or greeting with their silent askew mouths

sometimes would you believe it
i imagined myself as president of australia

ordering bloody aussies to open up
a great canal that runs right across australia

and turning australia into a
country of countries

with china in the middle
and every country else on the periphery

sometimes i simply spirit myself away
to more friendly places as far as the moon and mars

3

if i learn anything in australia
it is hatred nonchalance resentment jealousy
how to avoid human contact
how to dislike
how not to keep promises
how to give someone his professional minimum
how to be snobbish in interracial affairs
how to deliberately not notice certain things

how to forget one's existence

4

i do not love the moon any more
i like the sun even less
neither holds for me any illusion
of a bright future

here i am
living in a house made of time
that keeps missing things

if i have any space for breath
it is in my memory
of a pre-fragmented world

5

unmoved by questions like:
why did you come here
when do you plan to go back

i poured blackened engine oil
into the root of a gum tree
hoping that one day
a tree of total darkness
would shine like night
during the white day

6

already the critics are chirping
the editors are being made uneasy
in their easy chairs of power
of un/publishability

i found myself pressing these
words of poetry carefully
into a burial urn
like ashes of the dead
and did it like what they had done
to premier chou
scattering it on high
over the ocean the paddocks the rivers and hills
of an unwelcome cuntry

they are seeds
and will impregnate
a sterile land eventually

7

whenever i heard someone die by his or her own hand
i felt that he or she killed themselves for me
by extension the same blood had
coursed throughout our veins
and the instinct had been the same
even if the names and features
were not
as the last vestiges of a too-long civilisation
the face had no more value
to value
men prostitute their minds
women their bodies
the young their youth
the old their wisdom

expelled by our own brothers and sisters
we had come to other places of the world
to eke out a beggar's life
slaves of olden times
living only an imaginary equality

so when you kill yourselves
you also kill me
many many times

The Last Barrier

there is no racism in australia
only the language

the language of a people
rightly selected from the beginning

who closely embrace all the migrants
within the language

of departments dominated
by oxbridge

who know how to maintain
the purity of a language

of government officials
whose duty it is to be

linguistically correct
so that asian must not sound like asiatic

and celebrate multifacets of an ism
with this single language

of hard, and subtle, examiners
who know how to monitor the progress

of an examination
that started as early as the birth

of this nation
down to the last word:

oh
straight
liar

They Have Married White Men

somehow you can never catch their eyes
the most difficult thing the most shifting

it is other things you see often
the slightly exotic high-heeled shoes rarely seen here

the somewhat outlandish tight trousers
evocative of a past steeped in sexy sweaty humanity

and straight black hair
as memory long as shoulder

she for one as i could observe
felt a bit out of place in franklins amidst aisles of goods

looking everywhere and nowhere
except at myself

later i saw the grey-haired man
ten years her senior at least

whispering into her ear some humble things
while she turned her head elsewhere

gazing into the lens of a displayed camera
with a brand-new brand

or she who walked elastically beside her pink erton
a dishevelled man with a walking stick

down russell street
she was so unconsciously happy dressed exactly like a stripteaser

from an x club
that i caught her eye only for a fleeting moment

and understood it was all there:
the begging before the love-making scene

for the sartorial excitement
or she who swiftly looked back at me

while her man was calling someone else
in a payphone booth

her dark eyes
recalling such a distant history of forgotten desires

that i dreamed of caressing her red shoes
that she must have put on for so many times to excite him with

How Many Years Does It Take to Become an Australian?

let me work this out first for my boy:

it probably takes him five years to completely forget
his own language
and speak english at home
provided his mother is also able to speak that language herself

for her although she admires australians for their directness
in money matters
and their casualness in daily wear
she shall only learn one thing
perhaps by mistake
that they will keep aloof from us
so why shouldn't we do the same?

and i shall need only a few months
to acquire my australian citizenship
and feel acutely someone who has had a home somewhere else
once upon a time
in memory

Sojourners?

sojourners, they say, we all are
nonsense
i am no more a sojourner
than a multiple-translated word
that means the same thing
i had wanted to stay in australia ever since i came in
i grew to like its maddening quiet
its none too friendly people
its two days of doing nothingism in a week
its 'stupid ball' on tv
and i hate china with all the hatred that only a chinese could summon
who was born there brought up with the suffocating culture
i said to myself when i contemplated suicide
that i wanted to go away to somewhere else
anywhere else than china is infinitely better even africa
never to return
what is there in china for me
i'm not fit for an official's life
or anything else
chinese is the skin i wanted to shed
chinese is the blood i wanted to change
chinese is the rubbish i wanted to get rid of

and yet:
as i am going back to the hated country
i wave good bye to australia
a country that does not adopt me
and now both countries i hate
with a vengeance
anyway in china
i can at least find some consolation
in the perpetual misery
while in the hated australia
i can't even find happiness in happiness
meant not for me

Poetry Unemployed (a sequence)

1

going to bed at midnight
past midnight
well into midnight

going to bed with no one
as no one has not gone to bed

going to bed after a shower
with all the blinds down
all the curtains drawn up

going to bed in the dark
in the grave dark
in the dark interior

going to bed
thinking of an ad/venture
for tomorrows

convinced that the future
will be mine
only in the dream

2

what a new life
with all the new terms to learn:

new start
unemployment benefits
social security
children and family allowances
health care cover card
concession cinema
concession bus
concession gas electricity and water
austudy

and writing applications
has become

a full-time job

3

becoming useless at forty
becoming out of date
in a new country
becoming less and less sure of who i am
what i am doing here
why i am here
becoming uninterested in their money
becoming known to fewer and fewer

becoming a total self
eventually

4

clothes several years old
the car newly bashed
a treeless christmas

and we watched
endless
tv
for free

5

your calls were not returned
nor were your christmas cards

the space became increasingly critical

then with the summer
came the flood
of conscious rejections

from elsewhere

6

it's always the experience
that got you

or qualifications

so that the only wish you had in life now
was to turn yourself into

a standardised screw

7

words refused to flow
from the frozen bank of memory
poems were strangers
gone with transient cars
there was no pain
there was only the mute stare of an eye

that carries more than despair

8

poetry
oh poetry
buy yourself a fax machine
a mobile phone
register a business name
and treat them

with respect

City in Waiting

facing poetry
the words refuse to flow

when anger is gone
the heart lays in white ashes

the jester
was applauded for saying

i'm not living on the dole
while thrusting fire into his lungs

you were walking away
having heard him whispering to the kids

hidden among the crowd:
one of these days i'll…

Rediscovered Poems

'no i won't go back to china he told me'

no I won't go back to china he told me
why I asked
there's no why I just did not want to go back
even if I die in Australia or elsewhere overseas
I have always regretted that I was born in china
instead of other places even africa even
an island in the ocean anywhere is better than
China
no never ask me such horrible questions
China is for the rich the powerful the foreign
not for me
I was born in china but not for china
we were all born for other places
that thing in us forever calling alien places home
having found a home we become
homeless again
we are nobody anyway
to whom a translated name doesn't mean much
nor does a translated life
while he was saying this
I thought of traitors I thought of
the guy who bit the hand that fed him
I thought of the defectors…foreign embassies
he seemed to have guessed at this
for he said
friend, aren't we all traitors
who must betray the country of their origins
in order to merely survive?
we are a totally different species
from all the others

for we reject what we are
accept what we are not
and that done
we reject what was accepted as we are not
and accept what was rejected as we are

you understand?

(handwritten on 17/7/1993, rediscovered and typed up on 20/6/2022)

The Poet's Wife (2)

If there is anyone the poet wants to
    pick up on
it would be his wife

she never goes to his poetry readings
she seldom reads his poems
    even if she does
she has a lot of fault to find with
    them

sometimes she'd find him still at desk
    writing poems
after a long sleep at night herself
she'd say to him,

Are they any good if you
write so quickly?

one other thing she constantly
reminds him of is that

fame is no good and probably no use
whoever sees a real genuine person
seeking fame the way you do
the famous are always a bit crazy
sick in the mind
they kill themselves and their wives
I don't want to be murdered by a
    famous poet and live ever after
        happily in a literary history book

the poet has nothing to say to all that
dumb he is

(handwritten on 25/1/1994, rediscovered and typed up on 20/6/2022)

On an Australia Day

what can we – a chinese
    family – do?

I'm reading xu dishan as irrelevant
    to australia as the moon is
    irrelevant to the sun

my wife is reading The Ruined
    Capital before she soon
    falls into a sleep on
    the third-hand sofa

my son is reading Bear
    or What Do People Do All
    Day?

having sucked dry a heap
    of home-made ice-suckers

all our windows are shut
    against the 39°C summer heat
    a mindless azure sky
    with lower-edged trees

australia is where
I don't really know

perhaps when the news starts at 5.30
    on Ten
it will come alive

(handwritten on 26/1/1994, rediscovered and typed up on 20/6/2022)

'the west in the whale'

the west in the whale
is floating up to shore

lured by the world
of its own creation

the west in the whale
wishing for a vision

of whiteness forever
under the sun on the beach

the west in the whale
dies its own death in white

(handwritten on 16/4/1994, rediscovered and typed up on 20/6/2022)

'how is one going to change himself'

how is one going to change himself
    in his late 30s
I happened to think of this
when I was washing my feet
a little past midnight
when no longer anything is happening
except the regular on-and-off of
a loyal refrigerator devoted to ice

vaguely I remember a dream I had sometime ago
about the age-problem and how to cope with it
was it I who faced it or someone else
or both

I've seen people who tried it
jumping from body to body
living a life of infinite possibilities
supposedly

I've seen women dressed so youngly
that they looked more make-loveable than marriageable
except that they gave a face that had the
    surface of a hard nut
when they turned around to peer at you

I have
thought of many changes
change of my blood
then of my body
with my coloured skin
and abnormal teeth

even now as I'm gazing myself in the mirror
    of eternity
at my own hallowed image as a barbarian god
I feel bored
how can one suffer a life that is worshipped
with only worship
and see a sky printed all over
    with his name only?

in one's late thirties
one feels the need for a change
so one goes outside and suddenly
    becomes aware
that the newly mowed lawn of the neighbour's
is silent with the falling darkness
while in one's own rank garden that
has been neglected for weeks
in total abandon of laziness
crickets are so loud with their songs
    for the approaching autumn
that one is left wondering
why he should be bothered at all

(handwritten on 1/3/1994, rediscovered and typed up on 20/6/2022)

The Chinese Way of Writing

Who's the most conservative in
    writing in the world
you asked the question to your students
who answered
Chinese of course
they always write characters
and nothing else

no you said
let me tell you this
that we not only write
from west to east
but also from north to south
and east to west
that's how you all end up here
down on the bottom
in australia

they sometimes even write in circles
intelligible only to themselves

(handwritten on 3/2/1994, rediscovered and typed up on 20/6/2022)

'I often wonder about them'

I often wonder about them
why they are so curiously out of words
when engaged in any conversation
even if they are writers
why in seminars between public talks or conferences
they have to read from pre-written pieces of paper
why they can't do it the way we do
drawing spiritual sources from memory
intact from industrialisation and computerisation
why they look so boring talk so boring
gluing their eyes to paper and words
and always the word

is that because I'm just guessing
they believe that the word has such power
that to acquire it one has to
write and write and write
until he writes all his life into it
until he becomes the word?

but I'm still dreaming of the person
who is as the story goes the Great Talker
who can talk everything alive
without a piece of paper
and the best thing about him is that
when he stands in front of the class
all the most beautiful girls in the university
would flock to the front and look up at him
watching him delivering his oral art
watching
with liquid tongues hanging out unconsciously

(handwritten on 27/10/1993, rediscovered and typed up on 20/6/2022)

After Colonisation

coolie is gone and the coolie mind is still strong
nations   car/nations   in/car/nations
are categorised rationalised by multiculturalism
new things are happening   post   post   post
everything
post imperialism
post racism
post Darwinism
post Maoism
post writing
post shitting

we become fashionably serious by copiously
quoting homi bhabha gayatri spivak edward said
and many more unpronounceable names
our own heads crowded with footnoting habits
it's easy
just go to Document and double click 'footnotes'
    then ok
anything can become a livelihood
multicultural writing
post-something or anything
the more post the better
academics are the only way of life
boring fas/tedious auto-erotic
something like putting one's finger into one's arsehole
and then look and smell what's there on the tip
disgusting but always bear in mind:

argument you need an argument there
analysis no description mind no body
until you see the whole world is just
these two eyes and one head
full of empty words
that help them survive

Ah Men

(handwritten on 23/10/1993, rediscovered and typed up on 20/6/2022)

Colonised

yes we are
I mean I am
even my uneven teeth are
crying to be set right
my face becoming bleached
with daily milk
cheap white
bread
my snotty stuff I picked
out of my nose
is whiter than in china
and my semen
is paler
even my shit
seems white in the white bowl
I'm whitened so to speak—
but all the time
I'm aware
I'm doing this one thing
of writing this poem
of righting this whiting this
poem

and of colonising it
with english

(handwritten on 27/10/1993, rediscovered and typed up on 20/6/2022)

The Lonely Man

He made the sudden discovery that he has spent
All his life in solitude
By now, he has transitioned from an animal capable of surviving the cold
The heat, the dirt, the anger, the revolution and the sexual hunger in China
To the one capable of surviving solitude and boredom
In Australia
Having completed the great blood transfusion of life and culture
He often remembers his friends from afar

Those who exchanged a few letters but have since stopped corresponding
Those who grew up together when young but that won't grow old together
Those who disappeared for good after meeting only once
Those whose voice he can recognise over the phone but whom he has never met
Those who are so famous that he's familiar with, without really knowing
He sometimes looks in the mirror but hardly knows himself
Someone half old, half young, half Chinese, and half foreign
Finding it hard to even communicate with himself
One night, he didn't go to bed until quite late
And when he went to the glass door he saw there was a dim light outside
On closer inspection he realised that it was the moon that had
                              accompanied him in many places
It was not till then that he found the inexpressible sense of loneliness in his heart
That he found this loneliness accompanying him was the sense of literature
A desire to be put to death before one comes alive
To be put to death before one dies, and to be put to death before one
                              is beside oneself
Without wanting anyone to know
Just writing it down for oneself to read

Farting

i don't know if it had anything to do with australia but in this family of three farting is a fact of life when the father farts the mother will turn away in disgust and so will the son both laughing at the same time finding it quite a funny occasion better than anything they are watching on tv because the father always farts with a noise sometimes big and sometimes small when the mother farts it is more like a revenge that will make the father comment: oh go away, you stink and when the son farts it's a different matter altogether for he farts secretively with no preambles in a car in the family room before the tv. or at the dinner table before anyone realises it the stink already gets into the nostrils and it's so stinking that the mother will bawl: get out you and the father will bawl, get out you and the son will look dejested and mumbles, i'm sorry

sometimes when the father farts he holds out one of his hands in the shape of a pistol pointed at the son and farts like a bullet or if he has more than one farting noise to make he holds out both his hands and farts until the son runs out of earshot

once it is embarrassing to mention that when both the father and the mother make love one of them farts and that nearly spoils the whole thing if they have not already got used to it to such a degree that they soon recover from the amusement of it when the stink dies down

For Christmas in the Year of the Bird

we haven't got a tree
it's not the money but the mind
the thing is where do we put it
in a corner that's occupied by tv
or on a bed that has to be slept every night

there are other things we haven't done before
or have forgotten how to do now
like singing christmas carols
to whom do we sing these lonely notes
to ourselves?

certainly we have forgotten what it all means
despite the effort to renew the memory by all the newspaper columnists
is it because someone has died in order to be reborn on christmas eve
that days leading up to it are so desolate
with all the rich gone from the city like a big flood in retreat
and the poor sticking to their useless fireplaces
supposedly happy

or is it because of the quality of thinking that distinguishes you
from mediocrity that saturates festivities such as this
that casts you helplessly into a state of restlessness
in which you do not even know if you are an uprooted tree
wanting to be put back into the soil however alien it is
or a piece of cake to be eaten at your own expense

the summer is so bright with thoughtless sunshine
that birds all kinds of birds chirp away their ethereal life
without giving a damn about what time it is
knowing that if they do not seize the chance
the grass will grow green again
with the winter coming

An Old Classmate Visits My Melbourne Home

it was to the accompaniment of the creaking noise of the left door
that he got into my car
i was thinking of their lack of such things back home
and he was asking about the price
and concluded that four thousand wasn't really that much

we were on our way from the city to west heidleberg

i showed him around in my rented garden
he wasn't particularly impressed with all the rank grass
he was a businessman by the way
i took him in and made him a pot of tea
the kind that you bought at a chinese shop
but never had the flavour of a home grown one
on which he commented that he'd bring me some
when he visited me next time

my wife noticed that he hadn't brought anything with him
except half a pack of marlboro
which both of us dragged
i could have thought of buying another pack
since he was here
but my wife was busy preparing the food
a murray perch nice pork rib pink shrimps mushrooms
and we were busy reminiscing about the good old days
who was doing what in where
and who was the most successful

when the dinner came
he politely declined all the meat stuff
asking for only snow peas and vegetables
saying that he had had too much of that already back home
that he wasn't used to that kind of cuisine any more since the way of life
back home was much improved and seemed better than here

glancing up and down at me and at the interior of my three-in-one
bungalow
he said
pointedly
that yours is the worst i have ever seen in all my australian days

and that did it
in an outburst of rage
what did i throw at him but words that suggested that i was already a poet
a poet who had done quite a number of readings around the town
in english
and was an invited one, too

to his curious perplexity

later when he was gone
my wife said to me
do you think he understood what you said at
all he saw
in you and your melbourne home
was living poverty
and you were talking about poetry!

i sat and brooded

The Sky

Having been living for a long time under the red sky
I often find that my eyes are looking at the reverse side of the sky
and I often find a feeling in the eyes of the pedestrians desirous of
                                                            a change of sky

Oh, my heaven
When people open their eyes
I often thought their eyes are already another sky

A Simple Mathematical Equation

A friend called
to tell
that his wife was coming to Australia
from mainland China
for reunion with him

but he didn't
sound
pleased

I said to him
if his wife came
his freedom would be divided by two
each holding a half
if they had one kid
it would have to be divided by three
if four
by four
just a
simple
mathematical equation

my friend was pleased
to hear that
and said,
you might as well
put that down in a
poem

so that is
exactly

what I did

Self-titled

However black my thought is
my poetry is as black

however ugly I am
my poetry is as ugly

My Heart

Is not in China

My heart
is not in the West

My heart –
where is it?

My heart

is nowhere to be found

it is inside my chest

Simile

I write poetry in the darkest age of poetry
I write poetry in the darkest poetic age
I write poetry about the darkest age
I write about the age of the darkest poetry
I write the darkest in the age of poetry
I write the darkest poetry of the age
I write the darkest age of poetry
I write the darkest age's poetry
I write the poetic age of the darkest
I write the age in the darkest poetry
I write the dark in the ageist poetry
I write poetry in the ageist darkness

simile (see-mee-leh) – Italian, similar: a directive to perform the indicated passage of a composition in a manner similar to the previous passage; similarly (from https://dictionary.onmuic.org/terms/3161-simile)

Acknowledgements

'Anecdotes from Life,' *Law/Text/Culture*, vol. 2, 1995, pp. 218–225.
'For Christmas in the Year of the Bird', *Southerly*, autumn 1996, p. 151.
'Diary of a Crazy Contemporary Convict', *Antipodes* (USA), 12/1996, p. 132.
'The last barrier', *Siglo*, no. 7, summer 1996/1997, p. 9.
'They have married white men', *Imago*, vol. 9, no. 2, 1997, pp. 114–5.
'How many years does it take to be an Australian?', *Australian Mosaic: an anthology of multicultural writing*, eds Sonia Mycak and Chris Baker, Rigby Heinemann, 1997, p. 40.
'Poetry unemployed' and 'City in waiting', *World Literature Written in English*, vol. 37, nos. 1 and 2, 1998, pp. 65–68.
'Who's afraid of Les Murray?', *LiNQ*, vol. 25, no. 1, 1998, p. 42.
'The other eye', *Cordite*, no. 4, 1998, p. 9.
'The white Australian', *Kunapipi*, vol. 2, 1998, pp. 90–92.
'The other eye', *Cordite*, no. 4, 1998, p. 9.
'An old classmate visits my Melbourne home', *LiNQ*, October 1999, p. 68.
'The House Problem', *Muse*, April, 1999, no. 183, p. 12.
'Career counselling to a student of English', *Social Alternatives*, no. 3, July 1999, p. 65.
'A Job Advertisement in China', *The Age*, 20 March 1999, p. 10 (Saturday Extra).
'Reviews of my unpublished book', *Blast*, spring 1999, p. 40.
'Lines written at the Melbourne Mental', *Ariel* (Canada), no. 2, April 2001, pp. 124–128.
'Fragments of an evening walk' and 'Spring Festival, 1994', *Contemporary Asian Australian Poets*, eds Adam Aitken, Kim Cheng Boey and Michelle Cahill, Puncher & Wattmann, 2013, pp. 182–3.
'Invading Australia, a fragment', *Eureka Street*, published on Monday 1/4/2013, at http://www.eurekastreet.com.au/article.aspx?aeid=35718

www.ingramcontent.com/pod-product-compliance
Lightning Source LLC
Chambersburg PA
CBHW050253120526
44590CB00016B/2332